Contents

Five senses 4

Smelling and tasting 6

Nice and nasty 8

Outdoor smells 10

Indoor smells 12

Sweet and salty 14

Bitter, sour and savoury 16

Spicy and cool 18

Fruity tastes 20

Dinner time! 22

Word bank 24

Five senses

You have five senses.
They are seeing,
touching, hearing,
smelling and tasting.

Touching

Seeing

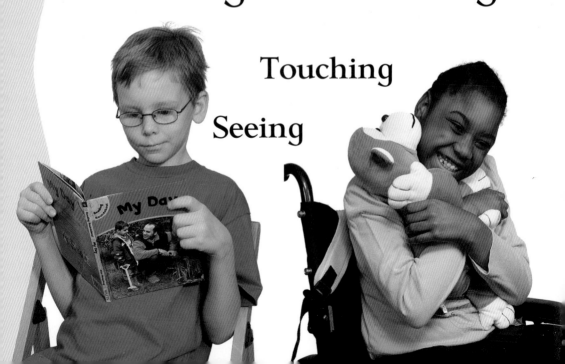

Smelling and Tasting

Paul Humphrey

Photography by Chris Fairclough

W
FRANKLIN WATTS
LONDON•SYDNEY

First published in 2007 by
Franklin Watts
338 Euston Road
London NW1 3BH

Franklin Watts Australia
Level 17/207 Kent Street
Sydney NSW 2000

ISBN: 978 0 7496 7452 6 (hbk)
ISBN: 978 0 7496 7464 9 (pbk)

Dewey classification number: 612.8'7

A CIP catalogue record for this book is available
from the British Library.

Planning and production by Discovery Books Limited
Editor: Rachel Tisdale
Designer: Ian Winton
Photography: Chris Fairclough
Series advisors: Diana Bentley MA and Dee Reid MA,
Fellows of Oxford Brookes University

The author, packager and publisher would like to thank the following
people for their participation in this book: Auriel and Ottilie Austin-Baker, Bryn
Stallard-Pearson, Harriet and Imogen Stanley, Lucas Tisdale, the students and
teachers of Penn Hall School, Wolverhampton.

Printed in China

Franklin Watts is a division of Hachette Children's Books.

Hearing

Smelling

Tasting

5

Smelling and tasting

You smell things with your nose.

You taste things
with your tongue.

Nice and nasty

Some things smell nice.

Some things smell nasty.

Outdoor smells

We like the smell of newly mown grass...

...and autumn leaves.

Indoor smells

We can smell
dinner cooking...

...and toast burning!

Sweet and salty

Mangoes taste sweet.

Crisps taste salty.

Bitter, sour and savoury

Rhubarb tastes bitter.

Lemons taste sour.

Cheese has a savoury taste.

Spicy and cool

Some things taste spicy and hot.

Some things taste cool.

Fruity tastes

Apples taste different to oranges...

...or strawberries.

Dinner time!

Sometimes we like to smell things before we taste them.

What is your
favourite smell
and taste?

Word bank

Look back for these words and pictures.

Bitter

Cool

Nasty smells

Nice smells

Nose

Salty

Savoury

Sour

Spicy

Sweet

Tongue